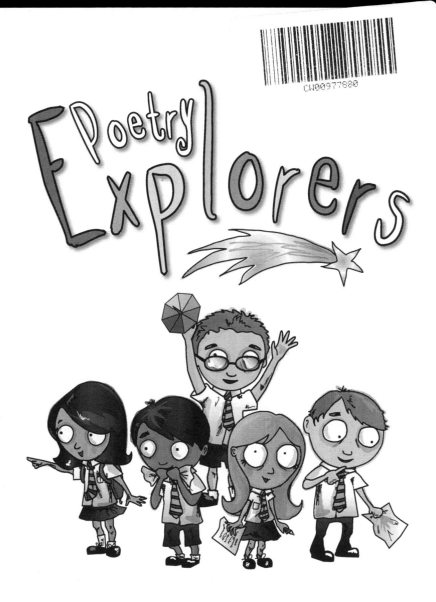

Poetry Explorers

Staffordshire

Edited by Donna Samworth

First published in Great Britain in 2009 by

 Young**Writers**

Remus House
Coltsfoot Drive
Peterborough
PE2 9JX
Telephone: 01733 890066
Website: www.youngwriters.co.uk

Foreword

At Young Writers our defining aim is to promote an enjoyment of reading and writing amongst children and young adults. By giving aspiring poets the opportunity to see their work in print, their love of the written word as well as confidence in their own abilities has the chance to blossom.

Our latest competition Poetry Explorers was designed to introduce primary school children to the wonders of creative expression. They were given free reign to write on any theme and in any style, thus encouraging them to use and explore a variety of different poetic forms.

We are proud to present the resulting collection of regional anthologies which are an excellent showcase of young writing talent. With such a diverse range of entries received, the selection process was difficult yet very rewarding. From comical rhymes to poignant verses, there is plenty to entertain and inspire within these pages. We hope you agree that this collection bursting with imagination is one to treasure.

Contents

Norton Primary School

Oakhill Primary School

St Andrew's Primary School, Stafford

St Anne's Primary School, Stafford

St Dominic's Catholic Primary School, Stone

St Matthew's CE(A) Primary School, Stoke-on-Trent

The William Amory Primary School, Stoke-on-Trent

The Poems

Breakfast With A Twist!

The evil hand grasps the polished, sleek spoon's stomach,
Constricting the bloodflow to his legs,
'Why me? Why me?' the terrified spoon screams,
'What have I done to you?'
Despite all protests, the hand tightens his grip
On the ever-wriggling spoon,
Unaware of all the commotion, the clueless cereal chants,
'Snap! Crackle! Pop! Snap! Crackle! Pop!'
Their usual cry for the roller coaster carriage to arrive . . .

Finally, the silver spoon appears over the horizon
Glinting in the sun,
All the cereals shout, 'Hooray!'
As it glides into the boarding area,
A mad scramble commences, as everyone wants a go,
After a couple of seconds, the spoon is lifted
And it goes up and up and up . . .

Adam Hunt (10)
Brindley Heath Junior School

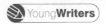

The War Of The Essentials

My hairbrush glides slowly through my hair,
Whispering softly in my ear,
'I'll be as careful as I can.'
The mirror watches over me,
Its gaze is almost blinding
And then he booms,
'I shine like the stars,
(When I am polished),
So clean me now!'
I exclaim, very loud,
My hairbrush reassures me,
She pats me on the shoulder,
I clutch my bag
And run away,
Not to be seen until later.

Molly Thomas (11)
Brindley Heath Junior School

Morning Madness

'Get up! Come on! Get up!' pestered my alarm clock,
He leaps, dives all over the place,
He bullies me until my hand stops it,
To my relief, it breaks,
My half-asleep body wanders downstairs,
Into the kitchen, where the friendless spoon squeals in fright,
As the milk conquers the cereal bowl in might,
The spoon is constricted in my podgy hand,
She holds her breath as she goes under,
But that is just the beginning,
She gasps for breath as she is plunged into the cave,
Her squinting eyes open out
As she is brought out into the light of the sleepy light,
He watches the spoon sobbing in the bowl,
Then simply chuckles to himself.

Edward Pearson (10)
Brindley Heath Junior School

Wild Weather

The sun wakes me up
With a smile in the morning.
The helpless houses get suffocated
By the fog, as it floats around town.
Splattering and leaping
The rain springs down
From the dying clouds.
The roaring, shouting and screaming
Thunder, terrifies children below.
Slowly, the gentle snow drifts
To the white, fluffy ground.
The terrifying hurricane tears
Across the countryside
Like a jet plane speeding.

Matthew Bridgewater (11)
Brindley Heath Junior School

Beans On Toast

'I'm awake! I'm awake!'
The alarm clock yells at ear-splitting volume,
As he dances and prances across the bedside table.

The impatient toaster roaring for attention,
As the crispy black toast springs from his metal head, sizzling
And gently parachutes his rock-hard crust and black beard
Onto my fine china plate,
The beans in the microwave, demanding to be released,
From the aggressive microwave,
Slowly scorching its tasty prisoner.

Finally released, the beans celebrate
And eagerly dance onto the crispy, black bed of the burnt toast,
Ready to fly into my famished mouth.

Harry James (11)
Brindley Heath Junior School

Weather

While the downpour gathers on the granite floor,
The dark black clouds leave the flooded town overcast.

Sprinting and darting, the wind bashes through the night sky,
The thunder screams in laughter,
As the lightning bolts flow through him.

The becalmed snow slowly melts when the sun starts to glare,
Over the town that is drenched from the downpour.

The unforgiving tornado tears through houses and barns,
While the sleet plummets to the destroyed town.

Nathan Webb (10)
Brindley Heath Junior School

Winter Weather

Drifting through the bare, frosty branches,
The snow coated the ground with a thick, icy blanket.
Floating gently through the bitterly cold air,
The delicate snowflakes parachuted slowly to the ground.

Whistling through the deserted street,
The wind sang its mournful song.
Sprinting and darting across the sky,
The cold wind seeps through your skin and seeps into your bones.

Thundering down and bouncing back up,
The rain falls rapidly in the storm.
Turning the crisp, white snow into slush,
The rain springs and jumps in the street.

Eve Pearsall (10)
Brindley Heath Junior School

Weather

The motherly snow,
Drifts and whispers gentle thoughts,

Jumping and leaping,
The rain springs out from the sky,

Smiling eye to eye,
The friendly sun greets me at the door,
She glances and glares at the people below,
As well as keeping them warm,

The gloomy grey clouds,
Crawl to cover the blue sky.

Claire Shakespeare (10)
Brindley Heath Junior School

The War Of The Furniture

'Come on! Come on!'
Yells the fire.
'Warm yourself on me,'
The sofa beckons.
'Come and take a break!'
The fireplace fiercely crackles
At the white leather sofa,
Which pesters me to sit on him,
As the fire warms me up.
I'm really unsure what's coming next,
But I know one thing,
This fight will never end!

Dominic Holt (11)
Brindley Heath Junior School

Wake Up!

'Wake up! Wake up!'
My alarm clock screamed,
'It's time to go to school!'
I reached out with hovering hands,
To pat him on the head.

'It's done! It's done!'
The toaster screamed,
As it began to jump around,
It squinted through the steamy smoke,
But there was not a sound.

Bethany Shanahan (10)
Brindley Heath Junior School

Teachers

Some are kind,
Some are quiet,
Some are loud,
Some are gentle,
Some are fierce,
Some forget your name,
'Dean . . . no . . . Tom . . . ah, yes, Joe,'
Some wear glasses,
Some are pretty,
Some are ugly,
Some are boring to listen to,
Teachers!

Joseph Ratcliffe (10)
Cheadle Primary School

Rose

Your little head, as red as blood,
Your spiky dress, as green as it could,
You stand out from the rest,
You really are one of the best.

But how could somebody pick you from your bed,
To prison you in a vase instead,
Can't they see you will never live,
In a vase their true beauty they can't give.

I would love you as you are,
You are my ickle super star!
So dance with the breeze,
In the garden, with the trees.

Your little head, as red as blood,
Your spiky dress, as green as it could,
Valentine's, birthdays and weddings galore,
But I think you say much, much more,
When you're left to grow on the garden floor!

Anghared Temple-Smith (11)
Cheadle Primary School

YoungWriters

Sound

If you listen carefully,
You will hear the sound,
Of the insect orchestra's first symphony,
Vibrating on the ground.

The squeaking of the clarinets,
The bows across the strings,
The beating of the big bass drum
And how the triangle tings.

Now, if you listen carefully,
You will not hear anything,
All you'll hear is silence,
Not even a triangle's ting.

You might hear the whooshing wind,
You might hear a shout from afar,
But you will not hear the insect orchestra,
For they just got crushed by a car!

Gemma Beth Mills (11)
Cheadle Primary School

Happiness

H aving fun with my friends and family
A nything which will cheer me up when I'm down
P erfect day with lots of exciting new things
P eople I don't know soon becoming my friends
I nside my own world of peace and quiet
N ever having a dull moment with my pets
E verything going well on a special day
S omeone saying nice things to me
S omewhere where I can chill out.

Rachel Ashworth (10)
Cheadle Primary School

My Sister

Big strops
Early bird
Dancing queen
TV mad
Big hugs
Messy room
Giggly girl
Pink dresses
And the best sister in the world!

Daniel Minor (10)
Cheadle Primary School

Music!

Music is a work of art,
Just like a piece of art.
The more you listen,
The more you like.
The louder the music,
The better you like.
Different types of music made now,
Brought to shops to sell.

Jordan Hollies (11)
Cheadle Primary School

Death

He's lurking in the shadows,
Waiting for his unsuspecting victim to approach,
His cape sinks into the shadows of sorrow,
He glides through the graveyard,
With his dark snigger following behind him,
His scythe hangs above his head,
So bright it would blind you,
His black, ancient cape covers his emancipated body,
His dark, voluminous hood, enclosing his treacherous face,
His bloodshot eyes reflect the moon, like lasers,
Keep your ears to the sky and your eyes to the ground,
Because you'll never know when Death's around.

Winner

Brittany Llewellyn (11)
Hillside Primary School

Teardrops

In a teardrop, I saw . . .
My favourite, most precious memories being stolen,
Nuns' and monks' heads spiralling round and round,
Fear in their eyes, as soldiers charged
Horrifically through the monastery.

In a teardrop, I heard . . .
Impacted armies heading towards us
To invade our only home,
The pounding of my heart
As my mind appeared to be
Moving closer to the edge of my shelter
I got more frightened.

In a teardrop, I tasted . . .
The tangy taste of dust floating upwards
And landing softly in my mouth,
Fear of death creeping through me
Settling at the back of my throat.

In a teardrop, I felt . . .
The extreme ending of my shelter,
The hard floor beneath me,
Heartbroken to see my final, clear night
Galloping away from me,
Twigs used to glide and pick me up
As though we were dancing together.

In a teardrop, I thought . . .
How I couldn't bear to see
Other nuns and monks suffer,
How much I would miss my family
And those I was leaving behind,
How I hoped God would be there
To answer my prayers.

Chloe Davies (9)
Hillside Primary School

13

Teardrops

In a teardrop, I saw . . .
The pure rage of the furious mob
As they ransacked through the monasteries,
Distressed faces of my brothers,
My brothers kneeling in silent prayers,
Deathly blood spread over the floor,
Like the tide coming in.

In a teardrop, I heard . . .
The thunderous bangs as the soldiers towered over me,
Gentle rustles of the golden, soft, silk altar cloth,
The colossal crash of the pure gold cross,
Soft goodbyes, as I cradled my wounded friend.

In a teardrop, I tasted . . .
The dry scent of fear,
Death as it was rammed down my throat,
Terror struck inside my mouth,
Like toffee sticking to your teeth.

In a teardrop, I felt . . .
The freezing cold stone floor
As a dagger dug through my soul,
The weight of inherited valuables,
Which I clung to anxiously,
As we scurried for survival.

In a teardrop, I remembered . . .
The blissful days when we prayed to God
In the shining sunlight,
The pleasant feeling of
Giving poor people food and shelter.

Megan Gregors (10)
Hillside Primary School

Teardrops

In a teardrop, I saw . . .
The radiant full moon drifting across the midnight sky,
The smashing of the door bursting open, like a cat through its flap,
My family and friends praying up to the floating heavens,
Nuns' faces as red as tomato skins.

In a teardrop, I heard . . .
Cries of loved ones carrying through the entire church,
Priceless valuables striking against the solid floor,
Henry's supply of warriors bellowing at me,
Like a tiger roaring in my face,
Whilst snatching the cross out of my arms,
God's angels chanting, as my family are going up to the Lord.

In a teardrop, I tasted . . .
Wave-like tears crashing against the bay of my tongue,
Congealed blood gushing out of my body.

In a teardrop, I felt . . .
The frozen knob of the door of death,
Precious items stolen out of my quivering hands,
Blood running quickly down my arms,
Just like the tears running down my face.

In a teardrop, I remembered . . .
That my hopes and dreams had been demolished
Just like everything that I stood for,
That God would have been satisfied with everything I had done,
That I have become mouldy, rotten
And that I am floating up into Heaven,
For I am now the guard and saviour of God.

Will Beech (9)
Hillside Primary School

Teardrops

In a teardrop, I saw . . .
The painful look on my brother and sister's faces,
My precious valuables being stolen from me,
The evil robbers snatching my things,
With a gang of knights behind them.

In a teardrop, I heard . . .
Screams of horror,
The rusty door being broken down,
Glass windows smashing,
Monks screaming,
As the soldiers burst in like lightning.

In a teardrop, I tasted . . .
Blood trickling across my face,
Sweat as it ran from my forehead,
I tasted fear in the air
And tears dribbling quickly like a cheetah running.

In a teardrop, I felt . . .
The cold whistling past my face,
Like lightning as the door smashed through,
The freezing cold feel of steel,
As the sword struck me,
The cold feel of rock, as I hit the solid floor.

In a teardrop, I thought . . .
About death and horror,
Wondering if some kind people will come to help us,
I desperately wanted them to go.

Brin Owens (9)
Hillside Primary School

Teardrops

In a teardrop, I saw . . .
The missing gold
That shone like the sun on a summer's day,
People crying, filling the room with water,
Like the ocean,
The arrows and swords left shining to Hell.

In a teardrop, I heard . . .
The heavy footsteps of Henry's men
Leaving with our men and women
As they tried to get the precious gold back,
The Devil's laughter going through everyone
Made us shiver like a fish out of water.

In a teardrop, I tasted . . .
Fear of the Devil
Like a red-hot chilli burning in my mouth,
The blood running through my veins
Like an Olympic runner running for the gold.

In a teardrop, I felt . . .
The plain floor that was damp
From teardrops that filled the room
Like there was a leak in the roof.

In a teardrop, I thought . . .
Of the golden cross that
Opened the gateway to Heaven
And my unfortunate family waiting there for me.

Sam Storey (10)
Hillside Primary School

Teardrops

In a teardrop, I saw . . .
My very precious valuables
Fade away into the middle of nowhere
My favourite vase smash
Onto the hard ground
Like lightning in the black sky.

In a teardrop, I heard . . .
The clashing of swords
As they fight like tigers
Leaping into action to catch their prey
The sound of crying from everybody around me
Puddles of tears
The dark night, crying like a tiny baby.

In a teardrop, I taste . . .
The fear of death
The taste of tangy tears pouring from my eyes
Like a water fountain.

In a teardrop, I felt . . .
My freezing cold face like snow
My mum's hand in mine.

In a teardrop, I thought . . .
About my brother and father
And the good times we had together
The thought of being in Heaven
With God.

Tilly Stair (10)
Hillside Primary School

Teardrops

In a teardrop, I saw . . .
A fierce gang of men charging after us,
As fast as lightning,
My precious valuables being snatched
Out of my shaking arms,
Woeful and weary people
Praying desperately for salvation.

In a teardrop, I heard . . .
The deep blue sea smashing and crashing
Against a humungous boulder,
People's screams and shouts,
Which fill the air with sorrow.

In a teardrop, I tasted . . .
The salty tears that dripped from my eyes
And the warm, fresh blood that drizzled from my nose.

In a teardrop, I felt . . .
The door of Death close in on me,
Scattered bones of the dead, which littered the floor,
The cold wind that blew through me,
Like a ghost lurking in the air.

In a teardrop, I remembered . . .
Delightful ties with my brothers,
Growing vegetables for the poor,
Endless days praying to God,
Who I know will be my Saviour.

Joshua Faulkner (10)
Hillside Primary School

Teardrops

In a teardrop, I saw . . .
The door fly down like a tree being felled,
Swords glimmering in the shining sun,
The gigantic army hovering behind them,
A tall, dead priest on the dirty, dusty floor,
With a dreadful spear to the heart.

In a teardrop, I heard . . .
Shouts of the men
As they smashed through,
Screams of the people
As they ran out of the horrid house
Away from the men.

In a teardrop, I tasted . . .
Fear hanging in the frozen, foggy air,
The tough taste of death in the bumpy streets.

In a teardrop, I touched . . .
The wonderful gold ornaments
That we had salvaged,
The frozen, cold, icy grass
As I fell to it.

In a teardrop, I thought . . .
Am I going to die?
The beautiful smiles of my lovely family
Filled my head.

Sarah Charlton (9)
Hillside Primary School

Teardrops

In a teardrop, I saw . . .
Men dashing at us like a tiger at his prey,
People shedding tears,
Praying to God to save us and our home,
The abbey disappearing piece by piece,
Men marching into the dark, black field.

In a teardrop, I heard . . .
The crashing of the doors
Being knocked down,
Screaming nuns
When things were being snatched fiercely from us,
Men bawling at us.

In a teardrop, I tasted . . .
Blood running down my forehead,
Salty tears dropping from my eyes,
Splashing into my mouth.

In a teardrop, I touched . . .
The scary black door of Death,
The cold, metal crosses.

In a teardrop, I thought . . .
God will save us,
The cross you will stand on in Heaven
And memories of my friends.

Catherine Butler (9)
Hillside Primary School

Teardrops

In a teardrop, I saw . . .
Windows being shattered into a million pieces,
Splinters racing across the room like bullets,
Nuns and monks clutching onto the gold cross
That lead up to Heaven
As they were dragged viciously away.

In a teardrop, I heard . . .
The crash of the monastery doors
Being ripped off their hinges,
Loud and blistering screams,
Echoing around the room.

In a teardrop, I tasted . . .
The gush of blood running down my sweaty forehead,
The salty taste of my teardrops, trickling down my petrified face.

In a teardrop, I felt . . .
The razor-sharp blade of a sword,
As it greedily plunged into my heart
And the freezing cold stone that hugged me
As I lay there in pain.

In a teardrop, I remembered . . .
My childhood memories
That zoomed past like cheetahs
And the pleasant sight of my brother's smile.

Ria Gabriella Johnson (10)
Hillside Primary School

Teardrops

In a teardrop, I saw . . .
The doors being bashed down
Like a plate being smashed into millions of pieces,
Dim, faint figures stealing marble
In wonderful great mounds,
Precious stone being sliced
In half and taken to the king.

In a teardrop, I heard . . .
The terrifying shrieks of the nuns and monks
Before they were murdered,
The roof toppling down
As if lightning had struck.

In a teardrop, I tasted . . .
The dry taste of fear sprinting through my veins
As I was pushed violently to the ground.

In a teardrop, I touched . . .
A burning blade
Piercing my soft skin
As I lay in horror.

In a teardrop, I remembered . . .
My family when I left home
How I had selflessly spent my life serving God
And all the friends I would be leaving behind.

Abigail Durose 10)
Hillside Primary School

Teardrops

In a teardrop, I saw . . .
That red, vicious star stabbing the light out of me
As multicoloured glass shattered down deep through the floor,
Doors being demolished, which led out to death.

In a teardrop, I heard . . .
The rattle of chains unleashing the army
Ready for battle,
Large screams zooming round my head, in terror.

In a teardrop, I tasted . . .
Salty water that trickled down my face,
As blood gushed out from my wound.

In a teardrop, I felt . . .
A razor-sharp blade plunge fiercely into me,
My shaking hands clinging desperately onto so many valuables,
That for many years I have lived with,
The freezing cold stone that hit me,
As I fell heavily to the floor.

In a teardrop, I remembered . . .
The graceful arms that my mother used to cradle me in,
As I screamed my first home down,
Images of my family, waving warm goodbyes,
Which will stay in my heart, forever.

Fern Massey (10)
Hillside Primary School

Teardrop

In a teardrop, I saw . . .
Smirking on their evil faces,
Dark, black knights charging
At the chained-up door,
Terror of death on their sparkling swords.

In a teardrop, I heard . . .
Knights clattering their swords
On the polished wooden floor,
Screams of friends and children,
Sounding like sweeping birds.

In a teardrop, I tasted . . .
Fear of wise men
As they jumped out of the window
In a flash.

In a teardrop, I felt . . .
A golden, glittering sword
Swarming on my fingers
As they were brutally severed.

In a teardrop, I remembered . . .
Those who mercifully survived
And sorrow filled my heart
For the brave men who died.

Konrad Pemberton (9)
Hillside Primary School

Teardrop

In a teardrop, I saw . . .
The door being thrown down
Like a bird swooping to catch its prey,
Soldiers slashing their swords, as quick as vipers,
Gigantic armies marching behind them
And a priest on the floor, with a spear to the heart.

In a teardrop, I heard . . .
Shouts of men as they crash through the colossal door,
Screams of nuns as they ran for their lives
And people praying as they went to Heaven.

In a teardrop, I tasted . . .
The strong tang of fear in the air,
Death as I ran for my life,
Blood leaking from my open wound.

In a teardrop, I felt . . .
The cold metal valuables we had saved,
The cold tiles as I was shoved to the ground.

In a teardrop, I thought . . .
Am I going to die?
As spears were thrown at me,
Childhood days ran by like cheetahs.

Aaron Dundas (10)
Hillside Primary School

Teardrops

In a teardrop, I saw . . .
Henry's men charging into our church
And ransacking all of our gold and chimes,
I saw a man with a brown hood
Stealing my solid gold cross.

In a teardrop, I heard . . .
Piercing screams of my brother,
The clattering sounds of the golden cross
Belonging to my brother.

In a teardrop, I tasted . . .
The fear of my brother
Running down my throat,
The salty taste of my tears.

In a teardrop, I felt . . .
The silver, sharp knife
Stabbing into my stomach.

In a teardrop, I remembered . . .
My father's face
And my mother's smile
I will never forget them.

Harry Clarke (10)
Hillside Primary School

Teardrops

In a teardrop, I saw . . .
The pang of fear on the other monks' faces,
The people tied to chairs,
Getting whipped on the spine by a chain.

In a teardrop, I heard . . .
Screams of death,
People sprint for their lives,
As the windows smashed.

In a teardrop, I tasted . . .
The blood dribbling,
As I licked it into my mouth.

In a teardrop, I felt . . .
The freezing cold wind blowing on my bare hands,
The freezing feel of steal.

In a teardrop, I thought . . .
Of my family being executed,
I remember my father's smile,
Showing his teeth.

Ronan Stevenson (9)
Hillside Primary School

Death

Death silently slinking into the shadows,
Bloodshot eyes scorched at his chosen victims,
Quietly, he moves closer and closer, through the darkness,
A cold-blooded killer, willing a victim to step from the house.

Kody Pemberton (10)
Hillside Primary School

Summer

Summer is great, sunny and hot,
Summer is great, I like it a lot,
Summer is great, we can all go away,
Summer is great, when we all go on holiday,
Summer is great, the birds singing in the trees,
Summer is great, the buzzing of the bees,
Summer is great, everyone is jolly,
Summer is great, no need for a brolly,
Summer is great, it makes everyone smile,
Summer is great, I hope it lasts for a while.

Megan Clee (9)
Hillside Primary School

It's Not Easy

It's not easy going out
Especially with all the flipping and faffing about
Doing hair, getting dressed
Picking a bag, doing make-up (unless you're a man)
In a rush, getting your dosh
What can I do? It's time to go
Oh no! As for your mum's shouting,
'Come on, you're being too slow!'
Thinking, *I'll make it quick!*
But is that really so?

Poppy Garside (10)
Hillside Primary School

The Beach

The silky golden sand creeps between my toes,
The sea delicately overlaps on the soft remains of a sandcastle,
Cliffs stand tall, towering over everyone and casting a shadow,
Buckets and spades sit lonely and abandoned
On the outstretched beach,
Rocks crawl and tumble over each other, swept up by the sea,
The wind howls like a wolf, demanding moonlight,
The sun glares down on the back of my neck,
Bringing a joyful feeling to my heart,
I am at the beach, a peaceful and happy place . . .

Reece Ford—Hulme (11)
Hillside Primary School

Bottom Wiggler

Constant cleaner
Fur gleamer
Glowing eyes
Hates surprise
Long leaper
Spider eater
Paw licker
Tail flicker.

Shannon Nicole Baddeley (10)
Hillside Primary School

Golden Gleamer

Golden glow
Dust show
Beaming bright
Yellow light
Day bringer
Shadow seeker
Winter stranger
Skin danger.

Megan Beardmore (9)
Hillside Primary School

The Volcano

My blood is the scorching lava, pulsing through my veins,
My voice is the *boom!* Of my angry eruption,
My bones are the rocky structure, holding me up,
My fury is the choking smoke, thickening the air,
My hair is the green grassland surrounding my base,
My victim is the innocent village below,
I will burn everything in my path,
For I am the volcano!

Callum Gater (11)
Hillside Primary School

What Is Love?

Love is your glistening smile lighting up your face
And the wind flowing through your hair
Love is a dove gliding through the air
And tweeting in the process
Love is a thousand stars piercing the night sky
Love is the first flower to blossom as a sign of spring
Love is a candle flickering on a romantic dinner table
Love is fuel to the world and to all mankind.

Katie Steele (10)
Hillside Primary School

The Wind

I am the wind,
My voice is the whistle of the wind,
My gaze is the blinding sun,
My clouds are blankets of air overhead,
My tears are rain, gently dropping,
My gift is the rainbow,
For I am the sky.

Jack Hudson (11)
Hillside Primary School

Death

Death, the cold-blooded criminal strikes again,
Regardless of age,
His dark, voluminous hood shadows his nebulous features,
As he glides silently towards his victim,
Blood-shot eyes glaring at his elected prey,
While they are blissfully unaware of their fate.

Emily Spencer (11)
Hillside Primary School

My Brother

My brother's a stealth bomber,
He flies without a trace,
His voice is an engine roaring and raring to go,
His eyes are exploding atom bombs bursting free,
If you try to stop my brother,
You'll be blown to pieces!

Alexander Oakes (11)
Hillside Primary School

The Sky

My voice is the whistle of the wind,
My gaze is the blinding sun,
My clouds are blankets of air dancing overhead,
My tears are the rain patting down my smooth face,
My gift is the rainbow,
For I am the sky.

Rhys James & Nathan Eagles (10)
Hillside Primary School

The Chameleon

He is camouflaged like a stealth bomber,
Concealed in any background,
His beady eyes are stars shining in the midnight sky,
His tongue stretches like an elastic band, ready to be released,
Silently, he hides in the bushes, ready to catch his prey,
His marks are colourful and weird.

David Mason (10)
Hillside Primary School

The Shark

His beady eyes are like shiny marbles, just polished,
His teeth are daggers, digging into its prey,
His fork-like tail is like windscreen wipers,
Swishing through the deep blue sea,
The deadly shark cruises through the dark gloomy ocean,
His skin is sandpaper, brushing against the rotting sea rocks.

Victoria Mallaburn (11)
Hillside Primary School

The Lion

His mane is a crown,
His paws are like boxing gloves,
His body is a tank, a killing machine,
Silently, he creeps up to his prey, like a gentle breeze,
His tail is a brush, sweeping away the flies.

James Clarke (10)
Hillside Primary School

Death

Death lumbers mercilessly towards his victim,
His hood dangling down over his treacherous face,
Bloodshot eyes staring at his prey,
As he awaits for his next death to occur.

Ashleigh Clee (11)
Hillside Primary School

The Earth

My voice is the rumbling sea,
My heart is the depths of the fiery Underworld,
My breath is the cold, depressing wind,
My eyes are the lightning of a storm,
For I am the Earth.

Georgia Mountford (10)
Hillside Primary School

The Lizard

His scales are luminous diamonds, glistening in the moonlight,
His teeth are like sharp icebergs, pointing like daggers,
He is a devilish trickster and a deceitful predator,
He is the king of the desert and the ruler of the sands,
He is like a sinister robber, hunting down anything in his path.

Hope Millington (11)
Hillside Primary School

Death

Death glides into the black shadows,
Mist moving around the graves, covering the night sky,
A cold-blooded law-breaker, willing a victim to step
From the dark, gloomy house,
His dark hood dropping down, covering his treacherous face.

Callum Abraham & Jack Grocott (10)
Hillside Primary School

Vines In The Jungle

Vine, vine, vine,
Monkeys swinging
Through the vine,
Tree to tree
Vine, vine, vine,
Rope suspender,
Vine.

Tree, tree, tree
Parrots squawking
In the trees,
Swishing, swooshing
Tree.

Rock, rock, rock,
Water crashing
Off the rocks,
Rocks, rocks, rocks,
Big, bold
Rocks.

Swamp, swamp, swamp,
Crocs snapping,
Swamp, swamp, swamp
Stinky, smoky
Swamp.

Liam Healey (11)
John Bamford Primary School

The Time Machine

My heart was pounding,
The curtain was about to open,
I didn't want to do the school performance,
I wished I could turn back time,
Then I realised,
I could.

I raced home as fast as I could,
Flung open my laboratory door
And stepped up to the machine.

I gazed at it in amazement,
When I switched it on,
A bright red light shot out the side,
I had never used it before,
I didn't know what would happen.

Speaking into the microphone clearly, I said,
'To the day of the audition list,'
I knew what I had to do next,
Jump into the red light.

What if something happened?
What would everybody else think?
I knew I had to trust my machine.

Slowly, I stepped up to the machine,
I couldn't believe I was doing this,
'Do it!' I told myself,
'Do it!'

All of a sudden, I dived into the light,
A dizzy sensation fell over me,
Illuminous colours swirling round,
Faster than fast,
Quicker than quick,
I was speeding back in time.

It all started to slow down, until,
Crash!

I seemed to fall out of nowhere
And everywhere seemed,
Silent,
There was nothing but
Silence.

I finally realised where I was,
In my classroom,
Children started pouring in,
In came my teacher,
With the audition list.

I had done it!
Travelled back in time,
If only everyone else knew!

Poppy Folland—Booth (10)
John Bamford Primary School

The Sea

Gentle whispers of the waves,
Sandcastles half made,
Birds singing as they sweep through the ocean,
Shells slowly moving into the sea.

Dolphins singing as they swim,
Sharks searching for their next meal,
Children jumping over the waves,
Fishermen fishing day and night.

The smell of ice cream through the air,
Crabs scavenging in the sand,
The frisbee's flying,
While adults relax!

Lauren Bailey (11)
John Bamford Primary School

Save The Jungle

Loss
Jungle, jungle
Please save it
Don't cut trees down
Please save it
Jungle, jungle
Gain.

Loss
Human, human
Please save me
I'll last 100 years
Please save me
Jungle, jungle
Gain

Loss
Human, human
Please save me
Don't cut me down
Please save me
Human, human
Gain.

Ruth Johnstone (11)
John Bamford Primary School

Dancing Means So Much To Me

Dancing means so much to me,
Tapping and stepping all over the floor,
Dancing fills me up with glee,
To hear the crowd roar,

I close my eyes and feel the beat,
Before soon, I'm up on my feet,
Jumping and skipping, circling the floor,
When I'm finished, I try some more,
Dancing is about being yourself,
Bringing something new to the floor,
Feel the rhythm, feel the beat,
Street dance some more,

Dancing's not about where you're from,
Or who's your mom,
Move your left foot, move your right,
You'll make a great sight.

Dancing means so much to me,
Tapping and stepping all over the floor,
Dancing fills me up with glee,
To hear the crowd roar.

Bethani-Lee Dalziel (9)
John Bamford Primary School

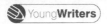

My Dog, Molly

Slipper stealer
Bone chewer
Face licker
Loud barker
Ball bouncer
Good friend
Treat teller
Lead puller
Bunny chaser
Food gobbler
Doggy paddler
Loud snorer
Bum sniffer
Tail wagger
Bone wrecker
Neighbour disturber
Scruffy body
Torch lover
Ball lover
Bottle chewer . . .
Bestest friend ever!

Emily Harding (10)
John Bamford Primary School

The Sea

The sea,
Cold, wavy sea,
Salty, deep,
Cold, wavy sea,
Tropical fish, seahorses,
Cold, wavy sea,
Tranquillity, coral reef,
Cold, wavy sea,
Whales, sharks,
Cold, wavy sea,
Dolphins, sharks,
Cold, wavy sea,
Crabs, mussels,
Cold, wavy sea,
Boats fishing,
Cold, wavy sea,
Divers, goggles,
Cold, wavy sea,
Sun cream, snorkels,
Cold, wavy sea,
The sea!

Shona McKail (10)
John Bamford Primary School

The Wolves

Graceful wolves,
With amber eyes
And silky, silver fur,
The pups playing,
The alpha hunting,
Howling by moonlight,
Fur whitened by snow,
The winter comes,

They find dens,
To keep them alive and warm,
But the pups are older
And the alpha dies,
Uproar is caused
And a fight begins,

The stench of death,
In the air,
But it is peaceful,
A leader is elected
And a new life comes.

Matthew Barrasford (11)
John Bamford Primary School

The Jungle

Beautiful sounds all around,
Whirling water,
Roar of a lion,
Chirping of a bird,
Crystal-blue here and there
A beautiful sight everywhere.

This is the jungle
Hear it roar
This wall of heat
Pushing me back
This is the jungle
It's the tropical world.

The waterfall crashing
Upon the rocks
The animals screaming
Can you hear them?
Shimmering water beside me
Beautiful creatures above
The wonders of the jungle.

Connor Pritchard (10)
John Bamford Primary School

The Mysterious Jungle

As day dawns on the eerie jungle,
Snakes slither,
Monkeys swing in the vines above,
As the long grass sways gracefully in the wind,
Sways gracefully in the wind.

Winding rivers,
Multicoloured tropical fruits grow high above,
Poisonous snakes slither in the grass below,
As the smell of dirt drifts past me,
As it crumbles beneath my feet.

Tiny insects,
Creepy-crawlies,
Red ants,
Lay beneath your feet.

Leaves the size of umbrella tops,
Hang from treetops,
The sound of people chopping trees down in the distance,
As darkness of the night begins to fall.

Jessica Bentley (11)
John Bamford Primary School

Midsummer Dream

The midday sun glistened on a quiet stream,
The blue as can be wind blowing gently,
I love midsummer, it's like a dream.

When I look up, I see the clear blue sky,
I see the clouds there, like floating cotton,
It's so clear, I can't believe it,
I love midsummer, it's like a dream.

Suddenly, I smell something, *poppies,*
The sweat smell of poppies from the neighbouring fields,
I love midsummer, it's like a dream.

The midday sun glistened on the quiet stream,
In the blue sky above, floats cotton wool clouds,
There was the sweet scent of poppies,
Carried from a neighbouring field,
By the light summer breeze,
I love midsummer, it's like a dream.

Samantha Rose Whittall (10)
John Bamford Primary School

Soldier

People saver
Brave fighter
Enemy killer
Sharp shooter
Peace maker
I am a soldier.

Alex Crabtree (9)
John Bamford Primary School

Things In The Jungle

Splash! Splash!
Goes the crystal water
Splash! Splash!
Look at it go!

Roar! Roar!
Screams the lion at his prey
Roar! Roar!
Don't get in his way!

Squawk! Squawk!
Says the parrot
Squawk! Squawk!
Let it go free!

Hiss! Hiss!
Slithers the snake
Hiss! Hiss!
Shouts the scary serpent!

Jay Mitchinson (10)
John Bamford Primary School

Who Am I?

A meat eater
A neck ripper
A fish catcher
A bone ripper
An ice breaker
A polar bear.

Daniel Pearce (10)
John Bamford Primary School

Snowy Day

White snow, white snow,
Its crystal glow,
It's quite a show,
White snow, white snow.

Crispy snow, crispy snow,
It forms to make,
The perfect flake,
Crispy snow, crispy snow.

Freezing snow, freezing snow,
Have some heat
And warm your feet,
Freezing snow, freezing snow.

Gentle snow, gentle snow,
Slowly falling,
To and fro,
Gentle snow, gentle snow.

Thomas Done (11)
John Bamford Primary School

Easter

E veryone is having fun
A fter Easter, everyone is depressed all the Easter eggs are gone
S pringing colourful flowers are all about
T ails bobbing up and down all around
E aster eggs hidden in the grass, one problem, none can find them
R abbits bouncing up and down in the tall, thin, overgrown grass.

Kari Lindsey-Smith (9)
John Bamford Primary School

49

Dragon

He spreads his leathery wings,
Each as big as a living room,
His body as large as a lorry,
His mouth spitting flames that lick his foes.

A gigantic silhouette,
Looming above small, innocent houses,
He wonders who will be his next victim,
Girl or boy? Man or woman?

He roars ferociously, but abruptly,
Making people scream and scramble,
Like tiny, squealing ants,
Beneath his petrifying shadow.

He laughs a cruel, powerful laugh,
Then soars into the night,
Leaving ghostly, pale faces
And wailing babies, sobbing children.

Amy Jones (10)
John Bamford Primary School

The Jungle

J ust a quiet hiding spot
U nder the sun
N ever go back to the real world
G o there for a vacation
L eopards pounce and claw
E very day.

Samuel Massey (10)
John Bamford Primary School

The Shimmering Sea

An eerie silence,
With waves crashing in the distance,
A quiet whinny of a horse,
Every so often, an eek of a dolphin,
Searching, searching for its family,
The sea is a magical thing,

An old, abandoned hut, with a forest behind,
With stables to the right,
That's where a warhorse patiently stood,
With a rusty saddle on its back,
The sea is a magical thing,

Tropical fish swimming around,
Eating coral,
Searching and exploring,
Looking at the sea deep below and far above,
The sea is a magical thing!

Brittany Rawle (10)
John Bamford Primary School

A Dragon

Flame killer
Flesh ripper
People stealer
Bone cruncher
Tree stomper
Egg layer
A dragon.

Daniele Tomassi (10)
John Bamford Primary School

The Jungle

The jungle
Tropical trees
And the mighty roar
The jungle, the jungle, the jungle.

A wall of heat
A crashing waterfall
And a roar that pops your ears.

Fresh, wafting air
Passing your scented nose
And a lion
That puts on a mighty pose.

Birds are chirping
Towards the sea
Where miniature crabs
Nip at your knees.

Josh Pykett (10)
John Bamford Primary School

A Cartoon

Parent annoyer
Child amuser
Child laugher
Child cracker
Baby crier
Child wetter
Child attracter.

William Wright (9)
John Bamford Primary School

The Jungle

Shimmering pools
The sound of birds chirping
Water crashing off a waterfall
Into the crystal-blue river
That's the jungle.

Slippery, mossy rocks
A wall of heat
Lion roaring
Snakes slithering
That's the jungle.

Wafting air
Flows in the jungle
Over the animals
And talking parrots
That's the jungle.

Stephen Tomes (10)
John Bamford Primary School

What Am I?

A meat fighter
A skin tearer
A teeth grinder
A human killer
A paw licker
A meat chewer
I'm a tiger!

Thomas Oakley (9)
John Bamford Primary School

The Sea

The sea
Sand softener,
Shell catcher,
Sound maker,
Pier breaker.

The sea
Boats are bobbing,
Seagulls are squawking,
Sea life is stalking,
Seaweed walking.

The sea
The frothy waves settle
The dolphins emerge
The sea.

Jordan Ostle (10)
John Bamford Primary School

The Minotaur

Pitch-black fur spread across its body
Half-man, half-beast
It hides in the shadows
Away from the society of Man

Pushed away from its homeland
Warriors, hunters claiming fame and fortune
Slaying his people, enslaving his tribe
Burning his village to the ground.

Michael Grimley (11)
John Bamford Primary School

The Sea

Swiftly the sea sways,
Seagulls echoing,
Dolphins dancing,
Children playing.

I see lustrous shells,
Sharks' fins slapping vigorously,
Crabs crashing through the sea,
Wind whistling through the air.

Boats bobbing up and down,
Sails blowing in the wind,
Children playing on the pier,
Mums eating ice cream.

Hannah Bentley (11)
John Bamford Primary School

My Dad Is A . . .

Crazy talker
Mad runner
Noisy player
Brick layer
Lazy sleeper
Floor sweeper
Loony tapper
Mad hatter
Most of all
My dad is . . .
Great!

Megan McGahan (11)
John Bamford Primary School

Time Traveller

Glittering, gleaming
Like a crystal road
Spinning round, round
Mysterious glows
In the distance
Bang! Bang! Goes the
Time machine.

Fizzing on the time machine
Gloomy squeals
Amazing sights
Popping up and down
All around.

Elliot Bird (10)
John Bamford Primary School

Dancing

D oing my best
A lways dancing
N ow other people dance
C ostumes sparkle everywhere
I ndependent dancing
N ow everyone is flexible
G reat fun for other people

M any people dance
A ll the time I dance
D ance!

Fern Conroy (10)
John Bamford Primary School

Ice Cream

Strawberry supreme
Chocolate chip
Vanilla ice
Raspberry ripple
Mint infusions
Cookie dough

My tastebuds are tingling

Cold and wet
Flavours tickle
In my tummy

I love ice cream!

Kaier Smith (9)
John Bamford Primary School

Top Of The League Match

Pick up the ball and kick it down the lane,
Chest it down and pass it all around.

Run away, cross it, striker shoots, puts it away,
Score goes up, the opponent's goes down,
The team's fired up and ready to play.

The parents scream and shout,
The manager paces up and down,
The linesman waves his wonderful flag,
The referee pull out his yellow card
And blows the final whistle
'We're top of the league!' they shout.

Matthew Savic (10)
John Bamford Primary School

Deep Down Under

Illuminous fish linger around the dark coral,
The crystal-clear sea,
The bright sun,
It reflects the happiness of the holidaymakers.

Dad's sunbathing in the unlikely British weather,
Kids making the most of swimming in the sea,
Mums getting the picnics ready.

Shark linger around the seabed,
Neat, wet blankets of saltwater up your feet,
Whirlpools of water made up of tiny, crystal-clear saltwater,
Glistening in the sunlight.

Bradley Crook (10)
John Bamford Primary School

Leaving Someone

When someone leaves you forever,
You feel alone and empty,
Your heart starts to wonder why,
It has happened to yourself.

I know how it feels.

When they're gone, you are heartbroken,
In the scary world, you're alone,
No family, no friends, just alone.

Trust me, I know how it feels.

Abbie King (9)
John Bamford Primary School

Seaside

The shimmering, clear, crystal sea,
The sound of waves trickle through the air,
The calm tide breathes in and out gracefully.

Magic.

Tropical rainbow fish linger around the sea,
Clownfish weave in and out of coral,
Sharks, whales and dolphins float alongside divers,
All around, peaceful harmony.

Magic.

Amber Bickerton (11)
John Bamford Primary School

The Sea

S wift, salty sea,
H umming
I nky-blue ocean
M agical
M ythical mermaids
E normous
R eaching
I nky-green sea
N ever-ending
G allant Neptune's secret kingdom.

Jorden Brass (11)
John Bamford Primary School

Gymnastics

Springboard jumper
Backward roll bumper
Warm ups, warm downs
Jump up, jump down
Do the vault, do the dish
We can all do this!
Jump round
Around and around
Step up and do your exams
Yes, you've now won a badge!

Chloe Frater (10)
John Bamford Primary School

Rabbit And Fox

Rabbit
Lightning, bounding
Nibbling, biting, gnawing
A bouncing mammal, a hungry growler
Chewing, ripping, shredding
Slowly, pouncing
Fox.

Jorey Evans (9)
John Bamford Primary School

The Jungle

T he part of the place
H appiness is all around
E xcitement is an adventure

J ungle is a happy place
U se a little faith and trust
N ever give up
G ood and fun
L et the fun last
E xcitement.

Erica Bould (9)
Norton Primary School

Puppies

Puppies are so cute
Puppies are so nice
Puppies play bite you and never make you cry
Even babies can play with puppies
And some babies adore them
Never harm puppies or dogs
Because they are so dear.

Keaza Nagie Wallis–Clarke (9)
Norton Primary School

Staffy

Strong
Time
C A reful
Faithful
Family pet
Energ Y.

Keeley Woolridge (10)
Norton Primary School

Summer Poem

The sun is bright
It's a lovely sight
It gives off a lot of light
It has a lot of might
People like to fly their kite
The sun goes down when it's night.

Laura Stevenson (10)
Norton Primary School

Dog's Life – Haiku

Dog barking loudly
Eating and sleeping all day
Dashing and fetching.

Callum Venables (9)
Norton Primary School

Ponies – Haiku

Ponies so pretty
Galloping softly down roads
Ponies so mighty.

Kelsi Wright (8)
Norton Primary School

Leaves – Haiku

Leaves are falling down
Leaves fall softly in colours
Leaves fall from the trees.

Bethany Guest (8)
Norton Primary School

Dinosaur – Haiku

Some are big and small
Some can fly and some cannot
Some kill and some don't.

Shea Foster (9)
Norton Primary School

Why?

Tell me, tell me, tell me now,
Where and when and who and how?
Why do we grow hands and feet?
Why do bullies always cheat?

Tell me, tell me, tell me now,
Where and when and who and how?
Why do trees grow so tall?
Why do leaves drop mainly in fall?

Tell me, tell me, tell me now,
Where and when and who and how?
Why does the sky appear so blue?
Why do we catch bugs and the flu?

Tell me, tell me, tell me now,
Where and when and who and how?
Why do we have friends and foe?
All these questions - will I ever know?

Olivia Hodgson (11)
Oakhill Primary School

Dogs Do!

Wet dribbler
Cat chaser
Ball catcher
Biscuit snatcher
Sofa chewer
Tail wagger
Hair puller
Fast runner
Loud barker
Pawprint leaver
Mud digger
Face licker
Bone fetcher
Ear flapper
A good mate to have!

Fern Cole (10)
Oakhill Primary School

Love

Heart breaker
Hand trembler
Tear jerker
Good kisser
Funny joker
Pulse racer
Flower bringer
Ring wearer
A person in love.

Chloe Snape (11)
Oakhill Primary School

Autumn

Flowers scarcer
Branches barer
Birds go further
Days get shorter
Feathers thicker
Hedgehogs sleepier
Pavements leafier
Barns are fuller
Orchards fruitier
Trees are prettier
Harvesters busier
Mornings mistier
Air is clearer
Winter's nearer.

Maria Ffion Briggs (11)
Oakhill Primary School

Bees

Honey maker
Pollen taker
People chaser
Stinger bringer
Water hater
Flower lover
Noisy buzzer
Stripe wearer
Wing flapper
A small animal.

Amber Lemord Gardiner (10)
Oakhill Primary School

Vald The Vamp

The night dead and sombre,
Silence fulfils the boundaries,
Fog approaching the night's sky,
A carnivore lurking behind.

An unusual ivory face,
Deep black hair of haste,
Large, piercing eyes,
Fangs you can't disguise,
As a vampire lurks close behind.

The sunset becomes too blinding,
So he leaves his foolish prey,
Climbs into his pit
And abandons this crazy day!

Lucy Woodcock (11)
Oakhill Primary School

Dogs

Furry friends
Postman hater
Playful creature
Noisy eater
Walk lover
Man's best friend
Face licker
Treat barker
Day sleeper
A good pet.

Megan Kelly (11)
Oakhill Primary School

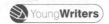

A Dog

Cat hater
All day barker
Walk lover
Food scrounger
Love wanter
Grown moaner
Fast runner
Ball catcher
Joy bringer
Milk drinker
Meat snatcher
Loud howler
Chop dribbler.

Sarah Keeling (10)
Oakhill Primary School

Olympics

Javelin hurler
Discus thrower
Top swimmer
Medal winner
Incredible runner
Extraordinary diver
Master archer
Healthy eater
Heavy weightlifter
Sword master
A really good athlete.

Alex Blackband (10)
Oakhill Primary School

Wood Elves

W onderful creatures, agile as a cat
O pen as a book being read every day
O ngoing and forgiving, like God himself
D elicate like a tree

E legant like the wind, swift and silent
L iving forever, like the forests they live in
V ictorious in their triumph for peace
E ternal wanderers with never-ending lives
S ilent whisperers, quiet and smart.

Gregory Ritchie (10)
Oakhill Primary School

Dogs

Bone fetcher
Stick chewer
Food eater
Cat hater
Man lover
Treat eater
Walk taker
Bad fighter
Dog!

Kyle John Bourne (10)
Oakhill Primary School

Jungle

Monkeys swing from the jungle trees,
They carry lots and lots of fleas,
Tigers hunt and prowl below,
While the moles dig in the undergrowth.
Marshy swamps in the heart of the jungle,
Dragonflies beat their wings,
While fish are waiting for them to drop,
The jungle is an amazing place,
It definitely is not a disgrace!

Jacob Fowell (10)
Oakhill Primary School

Animals

Digger upper
Messy eater
Loud barker
Dirty washer
Runner after
High jumper
Fast runner
Pillow shredder
Cat hater.

Macaulay Smith (9)
Oakhill Primary School

Dogs

Food stealer
Body biter
Messy eater
Slipper nicker
Loud barker
Sharp scratcher
Fast runner
Cat hater
Dog chaser.

Kayleigh Onions (10)
Oakhill Primary School

Space

Dream bringer
Silent sleeper
Air breaker
Dark bringer
Light hater
Vast sparkler
Love giver
Happiness wanter
It's all around us!

Matthew Haycock (11)
Oakhill Primary School

Space

S pace has no gravity
A stronauts built it
T iny compared to space
E arth put it there
L ots of information it holds
L ooks towards Earth
I nside are wires
T elecommunication devices it operates
E ntire object is made from metal.

James Keeling (9)
Oakhill Primary School

Football

F ouls, red and yellow cards
O range, black, red and blue kits
O pen goal is good luck
T all and small players
B ackpasses to the goalie can't be picked up
A mazing goal
L osers go in a mood
L iverpool are the best!

Chloe Hulme (9)
Oakhill Primary School

Space

Peaceful floater
Star watcher
Moon walker
Soft eater
Oxygen breather
Brave flyer
Great explorer
A very clever person.

Paige Olivia Riley (10)
Oakhill Primary School

Football

F ootball is the most watched sport
O livier Dacourt is currently on loan from Inter Milan to Fulham
O bafemi Martins is fast
T ottenham are in the Carling Cup Final
B erbatov plays for Man U
A ilton is the fastest person on the planet
L e Nou camp is the biggest stadium
L oony Rooney scores again.

Niall Bailey (9)
Oakhill Primary School

Unhappy

U nhappiness is when you have no one to talk to
N othing to keep you entertained
H oping your loved ones will come back to you
A lone, wanting someone to be with you
P aranoid, starting to realise what you have done wrong
P eople in your head calling you horrible names
Y ou feel you've let people down and made yourself
                                        an embarrassment.

Jordan McEvoy (11)
Oakhill Primary School

Football

Money makers
Best player
Injury fakers
Rough player
Ball snatcher
Red card
Injured player
Match winners.

Niall Shaw (9)
Oakhill Primary School

Autumn Fall

Orange, red and brown leaves,
Falling down from the trees,
As I walk along the path,
I can feel them crunch and mash,
Then the wind comes and blows,
All the bits past my nose,
Then the path is all clear,
Until the fall starts to reappear.

Georgina Tart (9)
Oakhill Primary School

Football

F ouled on red and yellow cards
O range, black, red, white kits
O pen goal
T eammates stick together
B oot the ball away from the goal
A mazing goal
L oony Rooney scores again
L oud crowd cheers us on.

Sophie Gilson (11)
Oakhill Primary School

Football

F un
O pen goal
O utstanding goal
T eammates stick together
B asketball is not my sport
A llowed to slide, but not two-footed
L oud crowd cheers us on
L oony Rooney scores again.

Ben Bradburn (11)
Oakhill Primary School

Dogs

Dinner eater
Loud barker
Good sniffer
Hard biter
Fast runner
Quick chaser
Treat beggar
A good friend.

Jacob Miller (10)
Oakhill Primary School

Space

Dark
All alone
The rocket flies
Up, up and away
Bye-bye Earth
Stars shining
Space.

Alex Woollam (10)
Oakhill Primary School

Me

Hard fighter
Quick runner
Game lover
Sweet chaser
Fruit hater
Dog liker
A good person.

Athanasious Allin (10)
Oakhill Primary School

A Rock Band

Head banger
Guitar thrasher
Gig lover
Pop hater
Strong rocker
Hair grower
Money maker.

Alex Taylor (10)
Oakhill Primary School

Rockers

R oaring crowd
O verheard miles away
C oncert fury
K errang! Concert
E lectric guitar
R eal rocker
S lipknot scream!

Thomas Keeling (10)
Oakhill Primary School

Brittany

Brittany
Helpful, friendly
Acting, smiling, laughing
My best friend
Giggling, shouting, singing
Lovely, kind
Friend!

Sophie Cooper (10)
Oakhill Primary School

Winter

W alls of bare leaves
 I n the house, playing around the tree
N ails waiting to be hung with presents
T all spruce trees covered in sparkling lights
E verywhere is glimmering white
R ed ribbon covering neatly wrapped boxes.

Thomas Grocott (10)
Oakhill Primary School

Friends

F orever and always
R ight by your side
I f you are sad, they cheer you up
E nding never comes between us
N attering is what we do best
D ie or live we are still bff.

Kayla Simpson (10)
Oakhill Primary School

Jaws

Human chaser
Head ripper
Bone crusher
Body cutter
Leg chomper
Blood sniffer.

Corey Varley (11)
Oakhill Primary School

Butterfly

A butterfly in the sky,
Up above, she flies so high,
Higher, higher, higher, high,
How she likes to flutter by,
What a lovely butterfly,
The caterpillar that can fly!

Katie Elizabeth Tart (10)
Oakhill Primary School

Stars

S tars shining brightly in the sky
T he sky shimmers with them in it
A stronauts talk about them
R ight where they are, it is perfect
S tars are lovely things!

Rebecca Thomas (10)
Oakhill Primary School

Water

W ater helps you to live
A ll drinks are made from water
T otally wet
E lectric jellyfish live in water
R ocks lie in the sea.

Jordan Brayford (11)
Oakhill Primary School

Hip, Hop, Hap, It's The Class Five Rap!

Emma, Henry, Lucy and Fin
Make their teacher jump in the bin

Megan, Tara, Sophie and Khi
Make their teacher eat a pea

Olly, Thomas, Nathan and Will
Make their teacher take a pill

Zoe, Toby, Gisela, Jack and Issy
Make their teacher really busy

Aaron, Jason, Siobhan and Zo
Give their teacher a big bow

Alicia, Ayesha, Henry and Jay
Make their teacher pay, pay, pay

Thomas, Megan, Anan and Nat
Make their teacher eat a bat

Eloise, James, Emily and Charlie
Make their teacher eat barley!

Isabelle Hyde (9)
St Andrew's Primary School, Stafford

Darth Vader

Darth Vader
And his red lightsaber.

On the old well-known sand planet,
They have no such birds as robins and gannets.

There isn't even such a thing as porridge,
Just Tuscan Raiders, strong and horrid.

As a child, a poor slave
And burnt by lava, a whole big wave.

Now Darth Vader, Lord of Sith
And he's a person, not a legend or myth.

He has fought droids and Count Doucou
And now he's joined the Dark Side too.

When young, very small,
Now quite big and very tall.

He goes Hodhu all day long
And in the Force, is very strong.

He's got a black helmet and a black cloak
And isn't very good at jokes.

On the Dark Side, big and strong
And if he hits you, the noise will be *bong!*

Toby Johnston (8)
St Andrew's Primary School, Stafford

Star Wars

Darth Maul
Had a great fall

Five Ewoks
Wore ten socks

Mace Windu
Went woohoo!

The Sith lord
Got very bored

Qui Gon Gin
Hurt his shin

The Death Star
Played the guitar

A droid
Got annoyed

Master Plokoon
Flew to the moon

Count Dooko
Did a number two.

William Marsden (9)

St Andrew's Primary School, Stafford

Hip, Hop, Hap, The Class Five Rap!

Rhiannon, Natasha, Oliver and Will
Make their teacher take a pill

Toby, Gisela, Zo and Zo
Tell their teacher, 'No! No! No!'

Jason, Aaron, James and Meg
Whack their teacher on the leg

Lucy, Henry, Emma and Fin
Bang their teacher with a pin

Charlie, Eloise, Shobhan and Soph
Give their teacher a big fat loaf

Isabelle, Tara, Emily and Thom
Give their teacher a bomb

Jack, Megan, Rhi and Nath
Make their teacher say a faith

Jay, Ayesha, Alecia and Thom
Attack their teacher with a pompom

Anan, Henry, William and Hen
Attack their teacher in a den.

Sophie Charlotte Thomas (9)
St Andrew's Primary School, Stafford

Zoz And Zoz's Pet Rap

Thomas, Jerry Mil and Pegs
Dress their owners up as eggs

Cookie, Spot, Sug and Spark
Make their owners eat tree bark

Crumble, Fluffy, Dust and Coke
Make their owners wear a cloak

Molly, Tara, Pump and Giz
Make their owners bang and fizz

Paul, Bob, Leo and Sam
Make their owners look like ham

Zoz and Zoz are very worn out
They've had a very bad day out and about.

Zoë Hall & Zoë Wright (8)
St Andrew's Primary School, Stafford

Planet – Haiku

Mars is so yummy
The stars sparkle in the sky
And Earth is *my* world.

Megan Washburn (9)
St Andrew's Primary School, Stafford

Diver

Come with me
To look, what you can see

Look over there, at that shark
That is swimming in a seaweed park

Wow, over there, a shoal of fish
Wait, is that a goldfish?

Ouch, a jellyfish
Hope I can make a wish

Now it's time to say goodbye to the creatures
I can swim back up to the beaches

That's the end
My dear friend.

Nathan Goodridge (9)
St Andrew's Primary School, Stafford

The Sea

Waves wash up on the shore,
Waves whirling, swirling, twirling,
I like the sea for sure.

The sand is scattered,
Lying around like rich gold,
Then the tide comes in.

Golden mermaids swim
And relaxing on warm rocks
And in their caves they rest.

Now you know the sea,
You can come and play with me,
From morning until half-three.

Emma Setterfield-Smith (9)
St Andrew's Primary School, Stafford

Star Wars

Darth Vader with his light
Stands up to start the fight.

If you go really, really far
You will find the Death Star.

Darth Maul against Qui-Gon Jinn
Darth Maul makes him lose his chin.

Obi -Wan Kenobi with his cloak
Makes Darth Vader drink his Coke.

One of the big, fat droids
Makes Mace Windu get annoyed.

Thomas Daykin (9)
St Andrew's Primary School, Stafford

Space

A ll I am is ready for a challenge
D ucking and diving, looking everywhere
V ery, very excited I am
E xploring more and having more fun
N ever have I been more ecstatic
T rials I have every day
U p, down, everywhere
R isky challenges come to me
O ver and over I go
U ndercover, no one knows me
S uperhero, that's who I am.

Lila Newport (10)
St Anne's Primary School, Stafford

I Love Animals So Much

I guanas to bats to elephants

L ike them all I do.
O f all the world's fantastic animals
V icious or tame will do
E ach and every one is special to me

A nd caring for them is my thing,
N ever being cruel to animals
I s a very important thing,
M aking the most of every day
A ll the joys the animals bring
L ife without them would be miserable,
S orrow would enter my heart

S ights and sounds of God's beautiful creatures
O ver land and sea, no area apart,

M y favourite animal,
U nlikely you can guess,
C rocodile! Predator, proud and strong,
H ope you like my animal poem, even if it's a little long.

Katharine Davies (10)
St Anne's Primary School, Stafford

The Dragon

The dragon
Very scaly
Breathing fire
Maybe red
Sometimes green
Long tail
Sharp teeth
Chinese symbol
Dinosaur related
Extinct now.

Cameron Hallows (10)
St Anne's Primary School, Stafford

Loch Ness Monster

Lurking underwater
Drowning pirates
Blue body
Long neck
Dinosaur related
Seabed shaking
Heavy weight
Decayed teeth
Stinking breath
Scottish beast.

Hayden Bush (10)
St Anne's Primary School, Stafford

A Mythical Creature

White body
Fluffy tummy
Snowman-like
Quite abominable
Looks petrifying
Gigantic creature
Mountain liver
Warm-coated
Two-legged
Massive monster.

Holly Hunt (10)
St Anne's Primary School, Stafford

Parrot

Colourful animal
Wonderful wings
Bird related
Tree liver
Large eyes
Black beak
Little claws
House pet
Fruit eater
Perch sitter.

Yvette Bentley (9)
St Anne's Primary School, Stafford

The Jungle

The jungle was full of colourful trees,
There were snakes, parrots, tigers and frogs
And on the trees there were hives, hanging full of bees,
Monkeys were swinging and lizards on logs,
Animals were asleep, not making a sound,
All over the trees hung long, dark green vines,
Cheetahs were running round and round,
But then it was sunset,
All the animals went to their bed and went to sleep.

Anya Elliman (9)
St Anne's Primary School, Stafford

The Jungle

Quick, quick, here comes a tiger!
Did that parrot just offer me some cider?
This jungle is such a pain,
I'm never coming here again!

Shoo, shoo, buzzy bee!
Ouch! Did you just sting my knee?
This jungle is such a pain,
I'm never coming here again!

Hannah Bennett (10)
St Anne's Primary School, Stafford

The Tiger Is Asleep

The tiger is asleep in the high bit of mountains,
The tiger is asleep in the river of fountains,
When he is awake he creeps,
In the morning he weeps.

At night he hunts
And in the morning he lies on his front,
His claws are sharp and long
And when he growls, his sound is nice and loud.

Dylan McKie (10)
St Anne's Primary School, Stafford

Space

Aliens hitching rides on meteors,
Planets wearing asteroid belts.
Astronauts discover planets and stars,
The rocks on Mars slowly melt.
Rockets racing like bats out of Hell,
Craters like huge wash basins.
Creatures with tentacles long and slimy,
Wrecked rockets floating peacefully along.

Andrew Lewis (10)
St Anne's Primary School, Stafford

The Jungle

Down in the jungle where the tigers roared
and the elephants snored,
the bees in the trees buzzed around
whilst leaves fell on the ground.
Frogs on logs,
snakes in lakes,
down in the jungle
the animals' place.

Isabel Harris (9)
St Anne's Primary School, Stafford

The Sad Day

S ome people feel sad today
A nd even I feel confused today.
D on't you even think that sorrow is an unhappy day.
N obody likes being so scared.
E ven I don't like being distraught.
S adness is a very unhappy thing.
S o are you feeling sad today?

Megan Francis (9)
St Anne's Primary School, Stafford

Dolphin

Dolphin,
Kind, fast,
Squeaker, fish eater,
Smooth-backed sea leaper,
Elegant tail swisher,
Sweet, shy
Mammals.

Alice Pennington (10)
St Anne's Primary School, Stafford

Mouse And Cat

Mouse
Little, fluffy
Quick, quiet, sneaky
Moves silently, sometimes not seen
Dangerous, scary, miaow
Big, long whiskers
Fat cat.

Abby Harrison (10)
St Anne's Primary School, Stafford

Elated

E lated is a good feeling
L onely is not an option
A dventurous is good when you're elated
T errified is not a good feeling
E lated forever
D elightful is good.

Jordan Smith (9)
St Anne's Primary School, Stafford

The Happy Poem

H ave you been smiling today?
A nd if you have that means you're happy!
P eople are blissful when they smile.
P eople are contented when they're full of laughter.
Y ou are elated when you feel good.

Danielle Radley (9)
St Anne's Primary School, Stafford

Stars

S hining bright in the sky
T winkling above the Earth so high
A ll lit up, so graceful and clear
R eally beautiful, I wish I could touch
S parkly stars, I love you so much.

Poppy Davies (9)
St Anne's Primary School, Stafford

Happy New Year

The ferocious tiger leapt left and right,
Dancing about in the middle of the night,
The animals were celebrating the happy New Year,
Also dancing were the deer.

The monkey was swinging in the trees,
Knocking about the sleeping bees,
He swung on a vine across the river,
When he reached the end he gave a shiver.

The lion was approaching, ready to pounce,
Although he was quiet like a mouse,
The lion's target was the monkey,
But instead he started to dance all funky.

'Two thousand and nine here we come,'
Shouted the lion, raising his thumb,
All the animals jumped with glee
As they all sat down and ate their tea.

Rebecca Smith (11)
St Dominic's Catholic Primary School, Stone

Terrified Tiger Trapped

The beast strolls left to right,
Looking through the bars so tight,
In the darkness of the stormy night,
Crying out with all its might,
This gave the birds a nasty fright
As the jaws clamped onto the bite.

People laughing, children gazing,
At the beast's stripes a-blazing;
As the beast took a bow into a rising,
The screams of many all so dazing;
As the shock of the stick flowing
The beast went down slowing.

Dawn breaks out; trees go to bed,
Without the beast being fed,
As it lowers its head,
And as the doors close on the rusty shed
All his grazing cuts turned ruby-red,
Just as his cranky mother had said.

As he tried to be strong,
Knowing it was all wrong
Listening out for this deathly dong
To paralyse him from his heavenly song,
He has lived too long,
(Was this where he should belong?)

Christopher Webb (11)
St Dominic's Catholic Primary School, Stone

The Old Man Of The Forest

Look at the green dotted around,
Each on long brown stems,
Some leaves dying on the ground,
Animals watching in their dens.

All the little insects burrowing underground,
The fruits in the trees sparkling like gems.
The birds in the trees making the most beautiful sounds,
Are the sparrows chattering to the wrens?

There in the quiet old wood,
Where the dark trees grow,
There a mysterious stranger stood,
Wondering which way to go.

Right in the middle of the cluster of trees,
The stranger looked around to the left and to the right,
And there in a cottage lived an old man, living so free,
Pointing him to the direction of the light.

The old man had a weather-beaten face,
With straggly long hair and sky-blue eyes,
He had been there for years without a trace,
Now with regret he let out a mighty sigh,
His secret was no more.

Dominic Shaw (11)
St Dominic's Catholic Primary School, Stone

Victory!

The weather raining.
The stadium stacked with supporters.
Crowd calling to their side.
The ball flies down the field.
The muddy pitch, squelching.
Covered with players.
The posts tall as cranes,
The ref calls for a penalty.
Tries can win a game.
Someone breaks through like a charging bull,
Crowd cheering,
Jump up like a Mexican wave.
The player dives,
A tiger launching at its prey.
The rain stops.
The sun shines.
Victory!

Tom Harvey (8)
St Dominic's Catholic Primary School, Stone

London

L ots of people
O n the train
N ot quiet
D oing fun things
O ver London Bridge, on a bus
N atural History Museum has lots of dinosaurs.

Joel Elliott (8)
St Dominic's Catholic Primary School, Stone

I Wish I Was A Mermaid

I wish I was a mermaid,
a tail that sparkles and shines,
I'd swim every single day,
with the fishy friends of mine,
I wish I was a mermaid,
with flowing hair of gold,
I'd giggle underwater
and never do what I was told.

I'd be the best mermaid,
in every single way,
Ariel would be my friend,
together, turtles we would save,
we'd swim with the dolphins
and dive and splash and play,
I wish I was a mermaid,
so I could swim every single day.

Francesca Elise Scott (8)
St Dominic's Catholic Primary School, Stone

Dragon

D angerous, deadly creatures of the volcano regions.
R unning thunderously through the magic forest.
A wesome creatures of the night.
G ruesomely tearing the flesh from its victims.
O vergrown vegetation he feeds off.
N otoriously famous for causing havoc.

Matthew Adams (8)
St Dominic's Catholic Primary School, Stone

The Mysterious Egg

One dark day, after school
Two young boys were by a forest pool.
Then they spotted something green
Not like anything that they'd ever seen.
It seemed to look like a glowing football
Why they went up to it at all is a mystery to us all.
They took it to a scientist to make it all clear
But even he didn't have the brightest idea.
Suddenly it started to crack
And they spotted something black.
It looked a lot like a small baby dragon
And had the tentacles of the legendary Kraken.
Then out of nowhere it disappeared
As the table was completely cleared.
From that day on it was never seen again
But I'm sure those boys didn't cause it any pain.

Christopher Paul Turner (11)

St Dominic's Catholic Primary School, Stone

Cycling

I enjoy playing in the local park
Because of dangers I come home before dark
I cycle sometimes on the road
But I'm always aware of the Green Cross Code
I wear my helmet in case I fall
Or it could be an ambulance to call!
When I arrive safely home I take my helmet from my head
Have a drink and go to bed.

Oliver Harrison (9)

St Dominic's Catholic Primary School, Stone

Tiger Trap!

A starry night,
With all the fright,
The people gazing,
The penguins dazing.
Colour fading,
The skin is shading.
The orange soon turned to white,
Losing all of his natural sight.
Peering through the bars,
Hearing all of the cars.
Hungry, he needs a bite,
But slowly losing all of his might.
Night falls,
The wolf calls.
Will he soon be free?
Is this the way it should be?

Emily Webb (11)
St Dominic's Catholic Primary School, Stone

Dogs

Barking mad in the street
All the dogs come out to eat.
Tall dogs, small dogs, black and brown
Panting, licking, sitting down.
People have us as pets,
When we're poorly we go to the vet's.
Best of all we like a fuss,
Chasing a ball or a ginger puss!

Paddy Harper—Scattergood (8)
St Dominic's Catholic Primary School, Stone

A Day In The Life Of Buttercup And Daisy

Buttercup and Daisy, such adorable rabbits
Soft and cuddly with fluffy tails
They hop around the garden with their funny little habits
But they run when it hails.

Floppy ears and twitching noses
Munching and crunching all day long
They love to eat the glittering roses
Sitting in the garden, listening to a bird's song.

A day in the life of Buttercup and Daisy
Always having so much fun
They are so crazy!
Run rabbit, run rabbit, run, run, run!

Olivia O'Dunne (9)
St Dominic's Catholic Primary School, Stone

Downs Banks

One crispy morning
We were still yawning.
It was muddy and slippy,
Oh what a pity.
The dogs were barking and larking,
There were places for parking.
People were walking
And people were talking.
Home for a nice hot drink
And dishes in the sink.

Megan Hanna (8)
St Dominic's Catholic Primary School, Stone

Snake

Slither is his name
A large slimy snake
Who lives in the reeds
Alongside the lake.

He enjoys sneaking around
Discovering food on the ground
His favourite meal is rats and mice
He could easily eat it twice.

His life is good
He has a scaly smile
He'll never be sad
He's a very cool reptile.

Christian Hallam (8)
St Dominic's Catholic Primary School, Stone

Snowman

Snow, snow, snow falling in my garden like cotton wool.
Need to wrap up warm and grab our coats
And start to build my snowman.
'Ouch!' Daddy and I decided to have a snowball fight.
'Wow!' Started to build my snowman, he's amazing,
Standing there in my garden.
My mummy's hat and my daddy's scarf.
A long carrot for his nose.
Now my snowman is complete,
Happy and glad that we can meet.

Daniella Bryan (7)
St Dominic's Catholic Primary School, Stone

The President

T oday
H ere on Capital Hill
E veryone gathered to witness history

P resident Obama
R ead his inaugural speech
E ach and every one
S tood and listened
I n anticipation
D eeply emotional
E xcited thoughts of a
N ew America,
T he new President!

Oliver Tinsley (9)
St Dominic's Catholic Primary School, Stone

The Poem About Bubbles, My Hamster

Bubbles is cute and cuddly.
He is very tiny and thin.
I pick up Bubbles and he nibbles me
So I flick him on the chin.
Round and round he goes
On his little toes.

Megan McLeod (7)
St Dominic's Catholic Primary School, Stone

Gabby's Gorilla

Peel flinger
Tree swinger
Flea catcher
Banana snatcher
Chest pounder
Roar sounder
Jungle god
Looks odd
Super strong
I'm not wrong
Beats his chest
He's the best!

Gabrielle Brindley (10)
St Dominic's Catholic Primary School, Stone

George

His name is George and he's my cat
And I love him so
My daddy accidentally weed on him
Because he bit his toe!
He's big and fat 'cause he loves to eat
And has lovely fluffy grey fur
And every time I go near him
You can hear him start to purr.
The one problem we have with George
Is he smells so bad
But I don't mind 'cause I love him so
And if he was gone I'd be sad.

India Webber-Clews (8)
St Dominic's Catholic Primary School, Stone

My Little Brother

Toy taker
Bath splasher
Puddle jumper
Early riser
Story listener
Bike rider
Hair wash hater
Block builder
Messy eater
Noisy shouter
Car pusher
A loveable boy.

Evie Hanscomb (8)
St Dominic's Catholic Primary School, Stone

Scruff

He is a little rascal, Scruff, my dog
Chews my toys and scrapes the walls
We go for a walk then he makes me jog
Chasing and catching bouncy balls!
I love the fluffy, lively boy
He brings me lots and lots of joy!

Callum Richard Plews (9)
St Dominic's Catholic Primary School, Stone

The Beach

B each is the join between land and sea.
E veryone's favourite place to be.
A lways fun and lots to see.
C atch the waves and swim the sea.
H ot or cold, the beach is where I want to be.

Emily Buckley (8)
St Dominic's Catholic Primary School, Stone

Snake

S ilently slithering
N asty fangs bulged with venom
A ir tasting with its flickering tongue
K illing and
E ating.

Sean Brown (8)
St Dominic's Catholic Primary School, Stone

Snow

I like to play in snow
To watch the beauty of it falling
To play and sledge with friends in tow
Then build a snowman and play snowballing.

Loxi Abbott (7)
St Dominic's Catholic Primary School, Stone

Seals

I love seals, they live in the sea,
I think seals are just like me,
They splish and splash and make me laugh
And they look like me in the bath!

Daisy Durn (7)
St Dominic's Catholic Primary School, Stone

Big Cats

Deadly hunter
Loud roar
Great pouncer
Midnight eater
Sharp claws
Sneaky creepy
Hairy, scary
Scratching trees
Deadly killer
White, brown
Sharp teeth
Throat ripper
Slow hunter
Meat eater
Large claw
Fast runner
Soft fur
Night-time mover
Day-time snoozer.
Big cats.

Sian Corbishley (8)
St Matthew's CE(A) Primary School, Stoke-on-Trent

Whales

Far traveller
Steady swimmer
Seal predator
Plankton eater
Smooth skin
Huge mammal
Squeaky voice
Song composer
Caring mother
Synchronised swimmer
Captive prisoner
Big fins
Aerodynamic, aerobatic
Tail slapper
High leaper
Sprays water
Splashes, thrashes
Sea lover.

Sam Humphries (8)
St Matthew's CE(A) Primary School, Stoke-on-Trent

Lightning

Lightning
Bright, very harsh
Crashing, falling, hurting
Demolishing all in its way
Lightning!

Olivia Watmough (10)
St Matthew's CE(A) Primary School, Stoke-on-Trent

Butterfly

Admiral flyer
Cabbage white
Doesn't crawl
Flutters by
Flower lover
Nectar thief
Delicate wings
Long-legged
Graceful dancer
Brightly coloured
Silent spy
Beautiful insect
Metamorphosis expert
Chemical defender
Spotty, stripy
Symmetrical patterns
Butterfly.

Bozena Evans-Coates (7)
St Matthew's CE(A) Primary School, Stoke-on-Trent

Red

My hamster's fiery eyes,
The ember of a fire,
The life support of a baby.
The lips of a lovebird,
Can be a comforting colour.
A sign of danger and fear,
A warning to stop.

Andrew Gunn (10)
St Matthew's CE(A) Primary School, Stoke-on-Trent

Rhino

Wild animal
African creature
Bull charge
Muddy-grey
Grass eater
Piggy eyes
Poor sight
Angry creature
Big, fat
Very speedy
Short tail
Short legs
Smells muddy
Pink tongue
Sharp horn
Rhino.

Charlotte Ellis (9)
St Matthew's CE(A) Primary School, Stoke-on-Trent

Pink

A nice sweet colour
A strawberry lipstick
A fluffy, beautiful colour
A girl band
A strong highlighter
A soothing smoothie
A colour of an animal
A type of ice cream.

Charlotte Goodwin (10)
St Matthew's CE(A) Primary School, Stoke-on-Trent

Cats

Slow stalker
Clawing walker
Fish breath
Light step
Mouse chaser
Sneaky racer
Orange tiger
Sharp biter
Dog hater
Sleep maker
Warm sleeper
Silent creeper
Spring pounces
Fast, bounces
Cats.

Lucy Hallsworth (8)
St Matthew's CE(A) Primary School, Stoke-on-Trent

Tiger

Speedy runner
Pouncing fast
Sneaky stalker
Grass flying
Deadly killer
Brown, white
Meat muncher
Glowing eyes
Tiger.

James Bloor (8)
St Matthew's CE(A) Primary School, Stoke-on-Trent

Golden Eagle

Majestic ruler
Loud screecher
Golden feathers
White chick
Powerful killer
Meat eater
Great flyer
Ripping beak
Vicious claws
Silent hunter
Hare, bloody
Deadly killer
Golden eagle.

Greg Lilley (8)
St Matthew's CE(A) Primary School, Stoke-on-Trent

Chameleon

Camouflage expert
Colour changer
Invisible reptile
Rotating eyes
Curly tongue
Fly catcher
Scaly fellow
Big crest
Sun lover
Fast runner
Chameleon.

Joshua Zikmanis (7)
St Matthew's CE(A) Primary School, Stoke-on-Trent

Dog's Life

Cat chaser
Postman biter
Paper chewer
Toy fetcher
Hunt leaper
Bone cruncher
Ball retriever
Race runner
Playing wild
Walk whiner
Water licker
Dog.

George Crook (9)
St Matthew's CE(A) Primary School, Stoke-on-Trent

Jungle

Spiders spinning
Snakes hissing
Lions roaring
Trees falling
Monkeys screeching
Elephants reaching
Noise and bustle
Quiet and tussles
Eating, sleeping
Laughing, weeping
All creatures
Great and small.

Ethan Walker (8)
St Matthew's CE(A) Primary School, Stoke-on-Trent

Haunted House

Creaky doors
Dusty floors
Chairs hard
Rooms dark
Chimney, smoky
Spiderwebs
Vampire nightmares
Ghosts dead
Quickly vanish
Loudly bang
Haunted house.

Brodie Owen (8)

St Matthew's CE(A) Primary School, Stoke-on-Trent

Kittens

Playful walker
Miaowing talker
Fish eater
Death cheater
Mysterious chaser
Sneaky racer
Dog hater
Fur ball maker
Comfort seeker
Purring sleeper
Kittens.

Summer Viggars (7)

St Matthew's CE(A) Primary School, Stoke-on-Trent

Hallowe'en

It was Hallowe'en night
I saw a little light
The door creaked open
I walked in
The door slammed shut
Something scratched my foot
I gave a shout
And fought my way out
Costumes all around me
Very, very freaky!

Aislin Leese (7)

St Matthew's CE(A) Primary School, Stoke-on-Trent

Snow And Rain

The
Snow
Snow is white
It is soft and cold
Snow falls gracefully
Rain falls hard and heavy
It is very dull!
Rain is cold
The
Rain.

Nikita Patel (11)

St Matthew's CE(A) Primary School, Stoke-on-Trent

Red Is . . .

A shiny, steaming racing car,
Fire in the darkness,
Pouring blood from a devil,
A bright scary colour,
A beautiful sunset.

Georgina Humphries (10)
St Matthew's CE(A) Primary School, Stoke-on-Trent

The Welsh Witch

There was a witch from Wales,
Who mixed eyes with puppy-dog tails,
Along came her mum
Who added a bun,
So then the potion did fail!

Jason Hallam (10)
St Matthew's CE(A) Primary School, Stoke-on-Trent

Agbonlahor Scores A Goal – Haiku

Agbonlahor scores
The goalie commits a foul
The whistle is blown.

Will Ward (9)
The William Amory Primary School, Stoke-on-Trent

The Amazing Butterfly And Wiggly Worm — Haikus

Rainbow-coloured wings,
The amazing butterfly,
Such pretty patterns.

Worms are so wriggly,
So pink and very slimy,
They wriggle all night.

Megan Alcock & Natasha Kirkland (10)
The William Amory Primary School, Stoke-on-Trent

Haikus

Football is a sport
Players practise on the pitch
Steven Gerrard rules.

Gorgeous chocolate
Chocolate as dark as night
Melting in the mouth.

Dominic Charlesworth (10)
The William Amory Primary School, Stoke-on-Trent

Wrestling And Football – Haikus

Rey Mysterio
And he does the 619
And a big frog splash.

Luke Rogers has scored
The goalie commits a foul
The whistle is blown.

Dylan Sammons (9)

The William Amory Primary School, Stoke-on-Trent

Chocolate Cookie And Strawberries – Haikus

Chocolate cookies,
Taste so great they melt away,
Leaving a great taste.

Strawberries so sweet,
Have one as a tasty treat,
Bright red and spotty.

Chloe Gerrity & Kaitlin Cornes (10)

The William Amory Primary School, Stoke-on-Trent

Rugby Player – Haiku

He runs down the wing
Dodging and running quickly
Fighting for the ball.

Jacob Walker (10)
The William Amory Primary School, Stoke-on-Trent

Friendship – Haiku

Hannah is my best friend
Me and Hannah forever
Best friends forever.

Layla–Leigh Dawson (9)
The William Amory Primary School, Stoke-on-Trent

Young Writers Information

We hope you have enjoyed reading this book - and that you will continue to enjoy it in the coming years.

If you like reading and writing poetry drop us a line, or give us a call, and we'll send you a free information pack.

Alternatively if you would like to order further copies of this book or any of our other titles, then please give us a call or log onto our website at www.youngwriters.co.uk

Young Writers Information
Remus House
Coltsfoot Drive
Peterborough
PE2 9JX
(01733) 890066